The Touch Of Life

A Collection of Free-Verse Poetry

Dr. Rithwik Rai

notionpress.com

INDIA · SINGAPORE · MALAYSIA

Notion Press Media Pvt Ltd

No. 50, Chettiyar Agaram Main Road,
Vanagaram, Chennai, Tamil Nadu – 600 095

First Published by Notion Press 2021
Copyright © Dr. Rithvik Rai 2021
All Rights Reserved.

ISBN 978-1-63997-515-0

This book has been published with all efforts taken to make the material error-free after the consent of the author. However, the author and the publisher do not assume and hereby disclaim any liability to any party for any loss, damage, or disruption caused by errors or omissions, whether such errors or omissions result from negligence, accident, or any other cause.

While every effort has been made to avoid any mistake or omission, this publication is being sold on the condition and understanding that neither the author nor the publishers or printers would be liable in any manner to any person by reason of any mistake or omission in this publication or for any action taken or omitted to be taken or advice rendered or accepted on the basis of this work. For any defect in printing or binding the publishers will be liable only to replace the defective copy by another copy of this work then available.

To my mother, who gave me life
And to my father, who continues to do so

Special Thanks

Dr. Sharika Sreeram

Dr. Seemitha Shetty

Dr. Vidhisha Shetty

Shreshta Bhandary

Dr. Abhay Bhat

Aakanksha Shetty

Karthik Rai

CONTENTS

Part I A Lifetime Ago — 13

1. Infinite Haze — 15
2. The Long Dream — 17
3. The Cruel Dream — 19
4. The Unspoken Night — 21
5. The Thirst of Desperation — 23
6. The Sleepless Night — 25
7. The White Soul — 27
8. The Whispering Past — 29

PART II Breathing Back to Life — 35

9. The Soul — 37
10. The Lion Heart — 39
11. Gentle Hands — 41
12. Growing Claws — 43
13. Painful Happiness — 45

14.	Fading Misery	47
15.	Warm Colors	49
16.	Nourishing Seeds	51

PART III Friendly Shadows   *53*

17.	Setting Sail	55
18.	Dreaming In Reality	56
19.	Flickering Light	58
20.	Negative Inception	60
21.	Purple Darkness	62
22.	Echo's From the Past	64
23.	Lasting Shadows	66

PART IV Darker Clouds   *69*

24.	Expanding Void	71
25.	I Am Singularity	73
26.	Unburnt Flames	75
27.	The Melody of Rage	76
28.	Shedding Light	78
29.	Closeness	80
30.	The Cold Night	82
31.	Rays of Hope	84

PART V Saving Light — 87

32. The Saviour — 89
33. Spirits of Future Past — 91
34. The Seed of Love — 93
35. Undeserved — 95
36. Shivers of Fear — 97
37. Rays From a Blackhole — 99
38. Colourful Blind Eyes — 101
39. The One? — 102
40. Melody of the Lullaby — 104
41. Wakes of Desperation — 106
42. Blind Fears — 108
43. Hurting Eyes — 110
44. Setting Sun — 112

PART VI Chasing Sunsets — 115

45. Debt of Love — 117
46. Beyond Bonds — 119
47. Peace — 121
48. Quest Full Eyes — 123
49. The Seeker — 124
50. I Hold On — 125

51.	Dream On	127
52.	Essence of Life	129
53.	Sunset	131
54.	Anonymous Answers	133

PART VII Purple Clarity — *135*

55.	Rains of the Past	137
56.	Children of the Soul	139
57.	Failing Ink	141
58.	A Foolish Mind	143
59.	Loving Pain	145
60.	Purple Wonders	147
61.	Unresentful Tears	149
62.	Smiles From Within	151

PART VIII Begin Again — *153*

63.	Waves of Love	155
64.	Strange Familiarity	157
65.	Beats	159
66.	Brown Eyes	161
67.	Brave New World	163
68.	Resonating Eyes	164
69.	Brown Resonance	165

70. Be Hurt	167
71. Three Beating Souls	169
72. A Blessing	170
73. Bleeding Tears	172
PART IX Golden Touch	***175***
74. Slipping Away	177
75. Skipping Beats	179
76. Flattening Lines	181
77. Cloaks of Love	185
78. Resurrection	187
79. She	189
80. Innocent Laughter	191
81. Hurting Bonds	193
82. Home	194
83. The Girl With The Golden Touch	196

PART I
A Lifetime Ago

INFINITE HAZE

It comes back to me
The oldest of the memories
I see hazes of purple
I feel her sitting next to me
I can see her talk
But I cannot hear her voice
Maybe my imagination
Is not strong enough to give her one
Or maybe it's some long lost memory
Seeping into my veins
Like the waters of Vienna!

It's nearly two decades ago
And yet it only feels like yesterday
Knowing what tomorrow holds
Life begun in death!

I can still smell the ashes

I can see the white colors

That stained hurting bodies wore

To keep their souls pure and intact

Do I miss her?

And if I did

Why do I miss her?

How can I miss something?

I never had

This makes me wonder

Does death really do us apart?

THE LONG DREAM

Vehicles passing by

People walking by

The scent in the air seems different

Yet it feels so familiar

At the same time much unknown!

Why am I being taken back?

Who is this holding my hand?

It's the same purple haze.

I see her eyes

They seem sad

Almost as if they are crying of pain

And yet she smiles

Every time she looks at me.

Maybe she sees the reflection of her in me

The kind of person she can be

Or maybe she's deciding to live again through me

Or maybe these are just clouds of judgement

That I tell myself

Every time I am made to travel to my past

In the quest to not find the truth

But just to perhaps live it once again!

Something that almost seems

Like a lifetime ago!

THE CRUEL DREAM

The room is dark

There's silence all around

Is there someone at the door?

Am I dreaming?

Whose hands are these that I hold so dearly

Nonetheless I seem to hold on to them tighter as the night passes by

I hold on to her hands

Tighter than I usually do

Something very comforting

In this darkness before me

Back then I did not want to wake up

But now I can't seem to wake up

Birds chirping at night

The sun is cold

The waves are silent

Is my reality all but nothing but a dream?

Waiting to be woken up from this obliviating darkness

Back in her arms

That were warmer than a thousand suns!

THE UNSPOKEN NIGHT

Why do I dream of reality?

Why is this anger showing me love?

I see her before me

They are flashes of light

That vaguely blind away the darkness

I feel her presence

Yet not her existence

I held her hand that evening

Letting go of it only for a moment

But she for a lifetime!

The sun seemed sad that day

The trees calmer than they usually were

The clouds all grey with no silver linings

And yet she smiled at me as I walked out the door
Or maybe that's what I make myself believe
Maybe I shape my memory into a brighter one
Wherein I tell myself that she did smile for me
Even though she held onto sadness in her eyes
Longer than I held her hand

Little did I know…
The only thing darker than the night to come
Was the lifetime ahead of us!

THE THIRST OF DESPERATION

I felt a thirst that evening

Only to realize two decades later

No water could ever quench it

My home, had just turned into walls and floors

The silent bricks gave me more answers than the people around

I heard the strangest voices

I saw the anonymous tears flow in people's eyes

I felt the shivers of men and women around me

Unsaid words began to scream!

And yet this little boy stood there

Only wanting nothing more

But a hand to hold

Now I wake up every morning

Wondering how that evening would go

Had I never let go of her that day

Perhaps then my dreams would be my reality

Or maybe this reality I live in…

Is nothing but a dream screaming to be woken up from!

THE SLEEPLESS NIGHT

The floor was cold that night
I no longer lived in my home
My life as I knew it
Had changed completely

I was not aware of what had happened
But I did feel it
Like a small piece of me had been lost

A child's heart may be innocent
But it sensed the change in the air
I was unaware of the outcome
But the wind spoke to me in whispers

I slept that night

With no hands to hold

At another's house

Because mine had just been destroyed

Little did I know?

The dawn of tomorrow

Will be a darkness in broad daylight

I slept that night like all children would…

Innocent

Unaware!

THE WHITE SOUL

The sun rose

Like it always does

Strong winds blew

The trees continued to breathe

It was perhaps the first that said…

Life goes on

I went back to my bricks and walls

And there she was…

Covered all in white

She was silent,

Still…

It looked like she was at peace

Now when I replay the picture in my head

But then again she had been silent for quite some time

Unaware of the seriousness

Blinded by the reality before me

I shed no tear

I felt no sorrow

Not because I felt no grief

But perhaps because this grief

Was not expected from a child

I started to grasp the reality

I was unaware of the concept

Of irreversible actions

Unchangeable circumstances…

Perhaps that day…

The only thing innocent that day…

Was my white soul!

THE WHISPERING PAST

She was great soul

She was as soft as the winter snow

She was as gentle as the sea breeze

Or so I am told…

She loved dearly

She held lovingly

She believed in you before me

Or so I am told…

Birth only has to end in death

But my birth started with death

I see them now

The hazes of purple she wore

I see the scarf she wore

The smile she wore

But I do not feel the pain she bore…

I do not see her…

I cannot feel her

They say she was mine

And yet I do not recognize her

She was taken from me

And all I have are some long lost memories

From what seems to exist

From a lifetime ago…

THE LYING TRUTH

As these ink drops fill in these pages
With the last few lines of this chapter

The purple haze that I continue to see
I thought I let go of it two decades ago

She was taken from me
And for that I forgive

I forgive the winds
I forgive the sun
I forgive the air we breathe
And the heavens we feel

All I have of her
Are blurring memories
Oblivious dreams
Anonymous voices

I told myself that these were enough

For me to hold on to love…

As these slowly began to fade like all memories do

Little did I know?

Of what the future held for me

My whole life written as a lie

Waiting to be unraveled

In the chapters ahead

This was all but a small chapter

Which began with love and innocence

Gravitating towards anger and hatred

Like a leaf falling to the ground

Surely

But inevitably…

The golden touch of life

Is nothing but a quest

Unraveling the tales of yesterday

Breathing the air of the present

And holding the vision of tomorrow

Waiting to be brought back to life!

PART II
Breathing Back to Life

THE SOUL

She left us divided
Into three broken hearts

One developed rage
One developed grief
And the other had only begun to feel

It seemed easier to give up
To stay down and turn into dust
But one brave heart
Held the hands of the other two…

He carried them through the storm
Into the light that he saw alone
Keeping her flames alive
He breathed us back to life

In us

He saw her light

She now lives on…

In him and I

For we were three remaining pieces of heart

One raging soul!

THE LION HEART

So here I was

Scent of a new place

New people around me

Everyone talked the same

Laughed the same

They even cried the same

And yet there was something different in life

I wonder what

This man who holds my hand

He looks happy

He feels afraid

I'm unable to figure it out

Is he afraid of losing what he has?

Or just sad from what he's lost

Yet he marches on

This man with a lion heart

He sees a future

That no one else can

Waiting to be molded

By this man with a lion heart

And I choose to hold his hand

For in him

I have begun to believe!

GENTLE HANDS

We look up at the heavens

In search of gods…

They save us from our miseries

They wipe the tears no one sees

Or so they say

I found mine

Walking amongst us mortals

This lion hearted man

Who faced the world

Holding the hands of none

But two young souls

The pain in my chest

Slowly seems to disappear

This fierce lion hearted man

Has the gentlest hands

I am able to hold them

And he doesn't seem to want to let go

He seems to slowly breathe us back to life

And we into him!

GROWING CLAWS

Years pass by

I sense the lion heart

He's getting stronger

He smiles because he wants to

Not because he has to

His laugh has the sound of happiness

He seems like a calm sea breeze

But I sense his pain

It's still here

But I also sense it fading away

Just like mine

But a lion has claws

And so we grew ours too

These claws pierce deep

We needed the radiance

To ensure these claws don't hurt

But instead caress

In the most gentlest of ways

But the claws were inevitable

And with them

Pain too was inevitable!

PAINFUL HAPPINESS

Have you figured it out yet?

How sometimes a hurting soul

Radiates with so much light

When you become one with the dust

You begin to see the grass

You start to feel its blades

Turn into trees!

Have you figured it out yet?

How happiness can be born

From nothing but pain and misery!

These smiles that I wear now

Have tasted the tears from my eyes

And yet the heart continues to beat

A little for itself

And slowly for another!

FADING MISERY

Breathing back to life

Seemed to feel like a realistic dream

Like a ray of light

During a walking nightmare!

Laughter seemed louder

Smiles began to grow

Like seeds blooming into trees

The long sighted dream

Began to slowly take form

The lion hearted man

Touched the innocent souls

The leap of faith

Pushed us from death to life

But the tale truly lies elsewhere

For family runs in veins

This chapter of the orange cloak

Was just beginning

A family created

From nothing but a smile

And a few words that held the universe ahead!

WARM COLORS

I was running that day

I can't seem to remember why

And out of the blue

Something caught my eye

Cloaks of orange

I stood there just for a second

And then she smiled

The smile that had the same warmth

As the purple haze

Little did I know?

That this color

Was here to nurture me

To shape my claws

And fill a void that was crying

In all its smiles!

NOURISHING SEEDS

Delusions are a tricky thing

They make you believe

The masks we wear perhaps

Are nothing but the truth!

We are sure

That these exist

This is the soul we bear!

Then one fine dawn

We are liberated from this

We begin to see

The path seems to clear out

For me…

It was that cloak of orange

She was no one

She could have walked away

And yet she stayed

Little did I know?

She was here to nurture the seed that was I!

PART III
Friendly Shadows

SETTING SAIL

Love was in the air

I slowly began to feel

This orange cloak

Truly has the warmest colors

To learn to give a little

Without expecting a lot in return

Helped me slowly

Shape myself into a happier reality

I was slowly beginning

To set sail on a journey

On happy waters

Sailing on this ship

That bore this colors of orange!

DREAMING IN REALITY

Laughter was here

I slept well

As I closed my eyes

And began to dream

Only to realize…

That even as I awoke

I continued to dream

Such was my life

There were no lines in between

The dreams were my reality

And in this reality

I learnt to live

As time passed

My claws continued to be molded

Kindness began to flow

In me and in the people around me

Or perhaps I began to see

What I had started to feel!

FLICKERING LIGHT

I wake up one night

Too good to be true…

Life can't be this good

Can it??

I began to question it

My reality

I began to question myself…

When you have known darkness

The way I have…

In time,

You will begin to question the light!

It was all well

And yet here I was

Beginning to fear the light

What if this light was not strong enough?

To keep away the darkness

My mind began to wonder!

NEGATIVE INCEPTION

Stay!

Don't leave me…

I screamed reaching out

To the orange cloak

And yet she kept moving apart

I see her hands reaching out…

And yet I can't seem to grab them!

A little more…

A little longer…

A little farther

I'm nearly there!!

My eyes open

Did I wake up?

Was it because I reached her hands?

Or was it because I did not?

The inception of negativity had begun!

PURPLE DARKNESS

I was not negative

I continued to believe

I was still happy

It's just that the air

Had an unpleasant direction…

The cloaks of orange

Never let go…

She continued to nurture!

But then it finally happened…

The day went dark

The truth finally crawled out…

I heard an anonymous voice

Whisper the truth to another…

The purple haze

My purple haze…

She was not taken from me

She chose to leave!

She had chosen death over my life!

ECHO'S FROM THE PAST

She chose to leave me?

The lines continued to echo

My life has been a lie

All the peace I made with reality

Built with pieces of a lie

Was I so bad?

That she chose death over me!

Or was she so weak?

That she chose death over light!

She chose to leave me

She was not taken from me!

Echo's getting louder

Even though they were only whispers

I refuse to let it in…

I tell myself that the anonymous voice I heard

Was telling nothing but lies

The purple haze had a gentle smile…

I continue to convince myself of that

She had a gentle smile!

She had a gentle smile?

Or did she?

LASTING SHADOWS

I spent years

Making peace with life

With my reality

With a truth…

That I was pushed to death

Only when I had begun to breathe…

Now they tell me

She was strong

And I ask myself

Since when did death show strength?

How can strength roar?

If it was born by walking away from life!

I tell myself now…

It's time to erase this light

Erase all that is bright

For they will all leave in time!

Just like the purple haze

That now I choose not to see

I walk now with my shadows

I embrace this darkness

And let go of all my light

For these shadows will forever walk by my side!

Unlike the purple haze

That chose to disappear into the darkness

And so now my darkness is born!

And will last me a lifetime…

PART IV
Darker Clouds

EXPANDING VOID

Alone…

I have people all around me

And yet this void

Only seems to get bigger

Human bonds

Are nothing but a weakness?

That are best severed

I am all I have

I am all I need

Humans are nothing

But vessels of service!

Use them as tools

Discard them as they blunt

Love is nothing but a weakness

That my darkness can no longer share!

I AM SINGULARITY

Give me what is mine

And I will bring you the universe

For I am singularity…

The center of this black hole

I am time and space

Nothing escapes my horizon

Not even the dying light

Edging into the depth of darkness

I am the condensate

Dripping down the glass of wine

I am the cigarette bud

Dying into the night!

Look up at the stars

Join the lines…

You come to realize

You are mine…

But I am no one's!

UNBURNT FLAMES

You can never be in search of something

If you haven't lost something

These emotions that I fight for…

Are the ones I need!

But the ones I rebel against…

Are perhaps the ones I desire!

This fire will eventually be lost

Forgotten in the sands of time…

But they may never cease to exist

Perhaps they were never made of flames…

These rebellious emotions

Shall only give me rebellious peace

But I accept this delusion…

Over the happiness of illusion!

THE MELODY OF RAGE

I have no tears…

My misery is a melody on its own

This rage I have.

Helps me conquer the world!

And yet I feel shallow…

In this deep sea of madness!

Love is a weakness…

Used by the weak

It only holds us back…

Why reach out to an emotion…

When all it does…

Is leave you wanting for more…

Hurting for more!!

Conquer this world

Use this fire…

Let go of people

Before they let you go…

For they are nothing but weak bonds

That will one day…

Drown you in this sea of madness!

SHEDDING LIGHT

I continue to use them
Those who give me love…
The cloaks of orange
Seem like a darker shade now
Stained by my rage
I notice it now…
So many wonderful colors around me…
Changing colors
Those who give me love…
They give me more than I to them
I give them nothing in return…
But pain and tears!

Yet I continue to believe
That my pain is bigger than theirs
For I was born in it!

I will continue to deceive them all…

All that they love in me

Is nothing but an illusion!

Of the image I create of me…

The image that you fall in love with…

So deeply and dearly

I too do not recognize it!

I am nothing but darkness…

This is all I have

This is all I need

I have shed all my light!

CLOSENESS

I am doing well

This darkness truly helps me

And yet

I feel hurt all the time

I do not fear it

My rage helps me mask it in the gentlest of ways!

I see everyone around me

They are just as miserable as I

And yet they try to better their lives

To better themselves

To hold on to love…

Such pointless emotions!

I have my shades of grey

That leans more to be black

Than it does to be white

But this keeps me away from love

And keeps me closer to me

The only thing close to me

Is I!

THE COLD NIGHT

Sleep not for the night is cold

The cold keeps you awake

But not alive!

For your fire has just begun

Stay close to this fire

For if not keeping you warm.

It will keep you alive!

In time…

This fire will grow

And it shall wipe out the cold

Sleep not for the night is cold…

The cold keeps you awake…

But not alive!

I continue my ways of life

I see myself tiring

Crying out for help

All in silence

But I stay close to this fire

For it keeps me awake…

But not alive!

RAYS OF HOPE

I am living this life

That is nothing but a lie

Trying to mask another lie

All that is real

Has begun to seem fake!

I have given up on them

Sadly…

I have also given up on myself

My fire seems to be dying

My eyes seem to be closing

Inch by inch…

Into eternal darkness

As they close

Edging into darkness

A ray of light!

Brightest of the rays…

My eyes find it hard to see

Then again…

They have lived in the darkness for so long!

I see the light now

It's beginning to take form

My eyes begin to open…

There she stood…

Sunshine!

Here to wipe away all the darkness

In me…

Around me…

Sunshine!

PART V
Saving Light

THE SAVIOUR

I thought to myself

As to how gentle I was as a person

Then I met her!

It was then I realized

I was nothing but a rebellious emotion

In a quest to shut my mind

As my eyes went to sleep!

Did I really start hearing the sound of the rain?

Drenching me in the summer heat

All this while…

My face cut out a smile

Whilst the people around me mourned!

Is she truly the girl with the golden touch?

Here to save my dying soul

Is she my saviour?

The one I was never in search of?

But the one I was blindly seeking

Is she the one to save me?

Is she my saving light?

SPIRITS OF FUTURE PAST

She touches my soul

Every time she holds my hand

Her light helps me see

Makes me want to believe…

The ghosts of our chained past

Often kill the free spirits of the future

They say all love stories

Are made in the heavens…

I ask myself

Then who does the devil marry?

My sins will never wash away

But I am learning to let them go

Learning to forgive myself

I was a dying light

That she chooses to liberate

With her sunshine!

A second chance?

THE SEED OF LOVE

Love is like a seed

It needs a little bit of sunshine

A little bit of rain

It needs nurturing

It needs some patience…

When it finally blooms

Recognize it for what it is

You can sow in deeper into the soil

Water it more than required

Shine out a thousand rays of light…

But it shall grow and bloom…

Only when it's time arrives

Take a deep breath

And feel the fragrance of its flowers

I am beginning to believe

In love…

In her…

In myself

She plants this seed of love

In me!

UNDESERVED

She makes me realize

Of how much I have been lying to myself

And the people around me

She seems so patient…

So calm

Nothing like the rebellious storm

That I hold within

She feels so warm

Gentle in every way

That a sinner like I…

Never deserves to have!

I am beginning to feel

I want her

I need her…

Yet I am not so sure…

As to if I deserve her!

SHIVERS OF FEAR

I am so afraid…

Of what I am beginning to feel

This beating heart in me…

Has begun to beat for another!

She is the light…

Here to save me from this black hole

That is collapsing

Due to its own mass!

I need her

I need her to save me!

I cannot risk dying again

But then again

If she were the one to kill me

Death over life!

I shall be reborn a star!

A leap of faith first

The trust later?

I wonder…

RAYS FROM A BLACKHOLE

The black hole…

The darkest entity known to exist

Nothing escapes a black hole

Not even the light!

The true irony lies in this fact

A black hole is nothing but a dead star

That radiated light for years

Light and dark

Love and hate…

Birth and death…

All originate from one point!

She makes me feel like I am reborn

A young new star…

My days as a black hole seem to be coming to an end

Her light was so strong

That it managed to escape…

The depths of my black hole!

COLOURFUL BLIND EYES

I slowly begin

To believe in her

In myself

She seems to numb out my pain

She says I'm numb

Little does she know?

Her smile is the one that relieves it…

She says I'm numb

Little does she know?

I'm beginning to find peace in her eyes

These blind eyes of mine

Are beginning to see colors!

THE ONE?

I am willing to take this leap of faith

Surrender myself to her!

This heart beats within me

Yet it beats for another!

I can see myself with her

I seem happy

I don't wonder if she's the one anymore

I know she is!

She is the one for me

The sunshine

For all my thunderous rainy clouds!

She is the one

My saving light!

Or so my heart says

I am beginning to feel convinced.

MELODY OF THE LULLABY

World's collide

Our hands held together

She saves me

Everyday!

I am able to rest

On her beating heart

She sings to the child in me!

I continue to fall deeper into sleep

Deeper in love

A crimeless sinner like me

Who never felt this love all my life

Her melody

Keeps my heart beating

I close my eyes

To the lullabies her heart sings to mine!

Fast asleep intoxicated by love

Never wanting to wake up!

WAKES OF DESPERATION

I am awoken

Yet again

Every night

I have begun to fear

Of how much I love her!

Afraid

Without her

I will be left back in pieces

Afraid without her sunshine

I shall enter into an eternal storm

That sees no return

And eventually be drowned in the sea of madness

That is my mind!

Yet I am unable to tell her

Of how much I love her

Perhaps this fear of departure

It's stronger than I thought it was

Stronger than me

It's keeping me awake

I lie awake

Yet again!

BLIND FEARS

She seems to be distancing

I was blinded by my fears

I was blind

Blind to her fears

Blind to the fact

That my fears are hurting her!

I want to get close

I am unable to do so!

What if she leaves

Like the purple haze

Who has begun to haunt my sleepless nights yet again!

The haziness continues

My unresolved past

Will destroy the light of my future

I can see her hurt

She seems to be losing her shine!

Am I the cause of this?

Am I sucking away her light?

HURTING EYES

I express my love

I express my fears

Yet she seems to be walking away

Now at a faster pace than before

Have I already destroyed her?

Has she now become a reflection of me?

Guilt is beginning to fill up my veins

I need her sunshine

Without her warmth

I'll freeze to death!

She's walking away

I try to reach out

My hands trembling as I do

Voice breaking

I finally reach her

She has tears in her eyes

I see her eyes

They seem hurt

They seem broken

I begin to see so much in her eyes

But I do not see the love!

Her eyes have lost the love they once had for me

All I see now

Are a pair of eyes

That are hurting

Please don't' leave me!

My selfish heart cries…

Please don't leave me!

SETTING SUN

I wake up

Yet again

Darkness fills my room

The silence is deafening!

So much pain within

I am unable to move my broken body

The sun slowly begins to rise outside

Yet it continues to remain dark

as tears flow down my face

Never have my eyes seen tears of their own

It was a new day…

A day without warmth…

For the sun had set for me!

She was gone…

No sunshine!

I shall continue to chase her

Through this storm.

For the sunlight from her setting sun

Is brighter than the rising sun I see!

PART VI
Chasing Sunsets

DEBT OF LOVE

Forever in her debt I shall lie

For there is no sin greater

And as the days go by

The weight of this debt rises!

This debt of love

I can never return

As time passes by

Further down I plunge into debt

Not realizing her sacrifice

Never expressing gratitude

Her silence

Always outweighed my anger

Forever I shall lie

In this debt of love!

BEYOND BONDS

When all your experiences

Pierce your heart

Like a million pieces of shredded glass

And you begin to lose the light

That your eyes once saw

You reach out for the reflection of the moon

In still waters

Remember the memories

That helped you smell a blossomed rose

In the desert of time

And that shall help you

Set free from all your misery

This bond

That is beyond all bonds!

I constantly find myself

Chasing shadows

Chasing reflections

But unfortunately

Fate has spoken

The past shall never meet the future

This is that sun

Which once set

Shall not rise

Gone are the days of sunshine!

PEACE

A day comes

In all our lives!

This world shall strip us

Of our love, hate, rage and misery!

Everything that we hold dear!

At that moment

Remember the smile

That brought peace to you

It shall cloak you

Keep you warm!

The layers of attachments and detachments

Will help you survive

She resides now

Only in my memory

I shall continue to chase her

In an ocean

That is a lost sea!

QUEST FULL EYES

Where do I look for her?

My heart yearns for her beat

I look around

I can feel her

Yet I do not see her!

The night seems to grow longer

It's freezing!

All I am left with

All this guilt!

I guess sometimes

Apologies are not good enough

My eyes are beginning to fade

I feel so afraid!

THE SEEKER

When the heart beats without ease
And the lungs breathe without any heat

When the sun seems cold
And the crashing waves make no sound

When you are in search of your identity
And you lose someone who you held close

You ask yourself; what is life?
You wonder; what is my purpose?

Across oceans and skies
Your heart beats for another
Perhaps this is my purpose
To beat for another!

I HOLD ON

I hold on

Just for another day

For another night

It's not that you were mine for me to let go

It's not that I was yours for you to hold on to

But there is something in me that is you

That tells me

Hold on…

Just for another day

For another night

Maybe the part of me that resides in you

Will one day

Wan to join back with the piece of you that resides in me!

It's not that it's hope

It's not that it's love

It's perhaps just fear!

Fear of letting you go

To such an extent

That one day you'll come looking

For that lost piece of you that resided in me

And I tell you that I no longer hold on to it.

So I'll hold on

Just for another day

For another night

I'll hold on!

DREAM ON

Dream on…

Till you become the dream!

I close my eyes

Hoping to find peace

That I never found in my reality

I hold within

Unwept tears of sorrow

This heaviness that I feel in my chest

Is nothing but the love I carry!

In time

I will be forgotten

But I continue to love

Over and over again

And then a little more

Love is the only thing

That keeps me alive!

ESSENCE OF LIFE

The essence of life
Is perhaps not life itself
But the fragrance of it

It's not the moment itself
But rather the thoughts and works
Leading to it
And remaining with us afterwards

Maybe it's not all flesh and blood
But rather the memories of the past
And visions of the future that we keep

Maybe that's why
Emotions run deeper than they did
Once the moment has passed!

I realize it now

The thoughts of the moments

Give me more happiness

Than the moment itself

Perhaps

I'm just chasing a ghost

That haunts me as beautiful memories

She's the past

A memory that has long set

After half a decade of chase

I think it's time I let her go…

Let her sunshine completely set from my memories!

SUNSET

I'll let you go today…

But only for this lifetime!

You are mine

In the life after this

And the one after!

I will go on till I find you

This soul I'm letting go now

Will go on till it finds you!

We may come back as hawks

Whilst your eyes will be hunting for prey

Mine will be in search of you

Maybe you'll come back as a deer

And me a lion

As I close in for the kill

I'll smell your fragrance

And I will slow down my pace!

You can come back as a peacock

And I'll be the rain

To whom you open up your feathers and dance to

Or maybe I will come back as your child

Then you will be forced to love me

More than any other

But we'll come back

Never again will we come as the sun and moon

One having to set for the other to rise

I'll come back for you

As I let you go

For this lifetime!

ANONYMOUS ANSWERS

Letting go of her

Was one of the hardest things to endure!

Each day…

Hurts

And yet I am breathing

The days seem long and tiring

The clouds above me

Blind my judgement

And just then

When I was at my worst

The anonymous voice

That spoke years ago

Speaks to me again

Sitting me down for the night

I was to be told a tale

A tale of the purple haze

That I was kept away from

The reality that was my hazed memory

It was going to be a long night!

PART VII
Purple Clarity

RAINS OF THE PAST

It's raining outside

The anonymous voice

That spoke years ago

Speaks again

But this time

To me!

Revealing the truth of my past

The voice carrier sits silent before me!

She is perhaps unable to grasp words

To begin the tale

Much like my failing ink in this chapter

I ask for forgiveness

A few emotions

Make every quill tremble

I am no match

For my hidden emotions

Are raging to explode

Thunder continues to rumble outside

Thunder rumbles in my heart

Anxious!

CHILDREN OF THE SOUL

She begins her tale

I sense her voice

She is hurting too

After all she and the purple haze

Both come from one soul

Sisters!

The anonymous voice

Was never anonymous to me

Only her words were!

She takes me to their childhood

Gentle!

Caring!

Warm!

Innocent!

The purple haze…

My mother!

Was nothing short of beautiful

My mind begins to question her future actions

Why?

FAILING INK

I am beginning to learn
Childhood
Even though it's in the past
It is the seed of our present
And the inception of our future!

One can never forget the past
Maybe by memory
But never by emotion!

Just the way hazes of purple
Had haunted my visions
She too…
Had inceptions of her past
That erupted and bloomed in her present
And incinerated her future!

I am at loss for words

Hoping my emotions will speak louder than my ink

For my ink is failing me…

A FOOLISH MIND

Bring me her soul

I used to yearn for it for years

Now here I am

Being told her tale

For the time

The world around me spinning

To a sober mind!

She pushed herself

For years

Fought her demons

Alone in the shadows!

The only thing that kept her going

Was us

But all love wears down

Due to the tides of life

I kept her going

And here I was thinking

She left because of us

She chose death over life

Because she felt she caused more pain than love

And an awake conscience is dangerous

Here I was thinking

She left me

Fool!

Such a fool I have been!

LOVING PAIN

She loved me

More than she loved herself

Or so I am told tonight

She wept tears of joy

When I was born

She wept tears of pain

When she let go of me

Or so I am told!

She loved me

More than she loved herself

Letting go of me

Had already killed her

Before she even closed her eyes!

I am told tonight

That love was all she had

Love was all she was

And I believe them

I believe her

I have begun to feel her faint beating heart

It beats…

For me!

It always did

I was just blind to it!

PURPLE WONDERS

Death does not do us apart
I am left feeling closer to her
That I ever have

The purple haze I used to see
Has begun to show clarity
Such a wonderful color!
Purple…
Such a wonderful emotion!

As I lay in bed
Thunder rumbling as it does
My body begins to shake
How could I not love her?
All these years

How could I not have missed her?

This purple clarity I see now

What is this?

Tears in my eyes!

My body shaking as I cry

I let go!

All my hatred seems to seep away from me

I feel my demons being cleansed

By the love that is hers

That has begun to flow in my veins

Purple love

Flowing in my veins!

UNRESENTFUL TEARS

Nearly two decades of emotion

Exploding all at once

She was beautiful

I spent years not shedding a tear

And now these tears

Do not stop

For they are weeping love

I have begun to bleed love

I spent years

Holding a clenched fist

And finally

I let go!

Such colors

The sun has begun to shine again

But this time

From within

I am so grateful

I am learning to let go

Without losing love

I shall love again!

SMILES FROM WITHIN

As I close this chapter

That had begun with hazes of purple

But ends with purple clarity!

I am taught to love

To continue to love

And to let go

Happiness may bring us peace

But pain brings us gratitude

If felt with the right heart

And seen with the right pair of eyes!

I will love again

I will feel again

I hold within me

A purple clarity

That teaches me emotions

Life never did.

I guess she never did leave me

My ink may have failed this chapter

These trembling fingers

Conveying emotions of purple clarity

Is an emotion in itself!

It's like a smile

From within!

PART VIII
Begin Again

WAVES OF LOVE

A life lived without love

Is a life yet to be lived!

Learn to love

A little stronger

A little longer!

In these flashes of life

Love is only but a moment

In these small moments

You truly discover yourself!

Learning to live…

With the acceptance of pain

Is in itself the greatest act of courage

Love with no bounds

And your soul shall reach the limitless heavens!

STRANGE FAMILIARITY

I was on my knees

Like I always have been

I weep no tears

For my eyes…

They are a desert

In between two oceans!

I feel this touch

Who is she?

Who holds me close?

It seems to me

Like I've known her eyes

For years now!

She's got a grace

That makes me want her more

Maybe she is the someday

That I had yearned for

Who has now come to be

My today!

BEATS

I begin again

One day at a time

One beat at a time

I have begun to smile

Not because I have to

But because I want to!

I do not see miserable people around me anymore

They seem like people filled with promises

Strength

With a will to fight

Layered with love

Slowly, but surely

I have started to live

And not just survive

Live!

BROWN EYES

Eyes!

Brown eyes

The minute I see them

Home!

My heart shouts!

Heart beats fast

My vision seems to blur

And yet…

My eyes are fixated on hers

Afraid!

If I were to lose contact…

I may lose her!

I've always been an afraid lover

Not afraid to love

But afraid of love itself!

This time…

My fear is not love!

BRAVE NEW WORLD

As I look at her
The world around me
Starts to fade!

The noises of the world
The words of people
The room seems to quiet down…

Every time my eyes meet hers
I find a new world
The stars shine bright here
The sun radiant in it's warmth

I look at her
And I see my heart
My moon and stars!

RESONATING EYES

Her eyes speak to me

They have the language of my soul

She resonates with my beats!

Something about her laugh

That speaks louder

Than the waves of the ocean!

Her smile radiates with warmth

Like that from the sun!

She's got all the colors of nature

For she is life herself!

BROWN RESONANCE

She asks nothing of me

She accepts my past

Something that took me decades

She so easily accepts it

Falls in love with it

Falls in love with me!

Her brown eyes

Took me nearly three decades to find

That streaks of brown in her hair

If god's blessings

Took a form

It would look like her

Just like her!

So many years have gone by

Her eyes are my home now

She's taught me to love

In a different way

In a new way

She redefines it

She's taught me to stay in love

To be loved

The colors from her eyes

They resonate with my soul

Such a beautiful Resonance!

BE HURT

Imagine…

Being in pain all the time

Having countless souls around you

Telling you not to be hurt

Telling you it will be all right

Countless number of times

They tell you

Repeat!

Then imagine

A pair of brown eyes

She tells me

Be hurt!

The world can take it!

I can take it…

She was not here to take away my pain

She was here to bear them with me!

Be hurt

I'm here

She says

Be hurt!

THREE BEATING SOULS

This heart of mine…
Now nearly moving past three and a half decades
Has learnt to beat in pieces

A small piece
Beats for me

A small piece…
Beats for my lady
Her brown eyes still continue to save me

And another small piece
Beats for the little piece of our souls
That grows within her
The three souls…
Beat in resonance!

A BLESSING

For years…

I was in search of a home

And now I finally have it

Her beating heart!

When I look at her

I realize

I always win

Even when I lose!

If it weren't for all the things I lost

I never would have won her!

Falling in love with her

Has been a privilege

Now she's giving birth

To a blessing!

BLEEDING TEARS

I hear a cry…

Such a beautiful girl

She has her mother's eyes…

She cries

The minute I hold her

She looks at me

I know she does not know me yet

But she has her mother's eyes

Such wonderful brown eyes!

I hold this piece of our souls

In my hand

Wiping her tears

As I wipe my own

For the love of my life

Is bleeding to death

She has always been a giver

Guess once again

She has given more than she could!

PART IX
Golden Touch

SLIPPING AWAY

The love of my life…

Drip by drip

Bleeds to death!

This is not justice!

I cannot be gifted with one pair of brown eyes

With another one

Being taken away from me!

One …

Breathing into life!

The other…

Out of life!

My golden hour

Is filled with beating hearts

One getting stronger by the minute

The other getting weaker!

Bring me life

I beg death

Do not visit me yet again!

SKIPPING BEATS

In these times…

Of nearing death

Life sure does slow down!

My mind runs back

To the first time

I laid my eyes

On her brown eyes

My dying lady

The first time

My heart skipped a beat

As it beat for her…

Now here she is

My home

Who gave me this child!

Here she is

Bleeding to death

It's a familiar silence in the air

I do not wish to think it

But I feel it around me

He is coming

My old friend

Death!

He is coming…

FLATTENING LINES

The line is flattening…

Or so I am told

Her heart is giving in

Or so I am told

Please god!

You have given me this miracle of birth

That I hold in my hands

All I ask of you

Is one more miracle

Save her!

But…

I am to be promised only one miracle

And that was the miracle of birth

Fulfilled!

Line flattens…

Heart stops beating

She's gone!

My heart continues to beat

But with no life

Death…

Could not stay away from me

Such was his love for me

Such…

Is the kiss of death!

UNSPOKEN GOODBYE

No goodbye…

No tears…

No last words…

Here a moment…

Gone the next!

I weep no tears

For death is my old friend after all

Even my life began with death!

I hold my child

Tighter

But gentler

She lost her mother

I lost a wife

We lost a home!

But I will

I will breathe her back to life

These tears can wait

For now…

Is the time to breathe ourselves back to life!

CLOAKS OF LOVE

Her eyes speak to me

Like words never have

An ocean of sorrows

Yet shining with a glitter of hope!

She'll love with a heart

That'll have bruised it's way through life perhaps

I'll cloak her with my warmth

That'll be brighter than a thousand Suns!

She may have hurtful nights

She may even hide her tears

But I'll see right through them

For I will always resonate with her sadness!

I tell myself this

Be kind to her

This love of yours

Will only be learning to love

To trust…

Hold her in your arms

Keep her close

For she is the one

Who will breathe you back to life!

RESURRECTION

I stand here now

Watching a red sky

As the sun sets before my eyes

Waves crashing at the shores

A familiar feel in my eyes to this sea before me!

I hold in my arms

The most beautiful pair of brown eyes

I have ever seen!

She breathes me back to life

I have lost so many people to death!

But the birth of this child

My child!

Brings them all back to life

She carries souls of my past

In each of her eyes

My beating heart

Is hers now!

SHE

There she is

Sitting with all her glory and warmth

She speaks ridiculously

But it makes all the sense to me!

She's the passionate kind

The one with the love that's warm and comforting

She's the impatient kind

But she makes me not want to make her wait!

She's the aggressive kind

She often speaks with no mind

But that's alright…

For she is all heart

And it's her heart that I will always protect

Always love

Madly, completely, unconditionally!

INNOCENT LAUGHTER

I often wonder

As these years pass by

As how to how one person

Can bring me the whole world!

Nearly four decades into my life

My past

Seems like a lifetime ago!

I stand here

Looking at the same sea

That I looked at

Years ago

Standing right here

Having lost the love of my life!

As I stand here

I feel the tight grip on my hand

It tightens with every wave

She laughs at the sea

Such innocence in her laughter

And I laugh because of her

For her…

My child!

HURTING BONDS

She makes me not want to hurt
She makes me want to smile
And not just smile because I need to!

She seems to hurt just like me at times
Every time she laughs or smiles
I see the shade of pain in her eyes!

I will always be there for her
Hold her by her hand
Aspiring for her happiness
Whilst we share our shades of sadness!

HOME

Years pass by…

Like seasons in the sky

I sit here now

Five decades into my life

Looking at the same sea

The same waves

The same sunset

They do not seem to age

I see her

Walking towards me

She's dressed in purple

Such a wonderful color

Such a wonderful emotion

She comes close

Smiling like she always does

Her beautiful brown eyes

Such a wonderful color

Such a wonderful soul!

She glows in this sunset

She keeps them all alive

She keeps me alive!

THE GIRL WITH THE GOLDEN TOUCH

She sits by my side

Holding my hands…

I feel the presence of three souls

In her warm hands

Dressed in the colors of purple

And her beautiful brown eyes

I cannot help but shed a tear!

My daughter

Holds them all!

I wondered all my life

I searched all my life

For the person

Who carried with them this touch…

This golden touch…

I wondered as to who held that touch!

It was her!

As she holds my hands

As we look at the setting sun

I know now

I did not save her

She saved me

She saved us all

This girl…

With a golden touch of life!

My girl with the golden touch of life!

The End

Printed in Great Britain
by Amazon